Read The Room

A Tarot Guide for Women Who Mean Business

Robyn Sayles

This book is dedicated to every brilliant, sarcastic weirdo who has ever scanned the shelves of business advice books and thought, "There has to be a different way to do this." To those who color outside the lines, march to the beat of their own drum, and aren't afraid to embrace the unconventional – this one's for you. May you find the wisdom and inspiration you seek, and may your path be uniquely and wonderfully your own.

Introduction

"You've always had the power..."
Glinda, The Wizard of Oz (1939)

Imagine, for a moment, that your brand is a lush, sprawling garden. You've planted seeds of vision, watered them with hard work, and nurtured them with love. But let's be real—sometimes, the garden of entrepreneurship feels more like a jungle. You're hacking through the underbrush of decisions, dodging the quicksand of market trends, and climbing the vines of team dynamics. What if I told you there's a magical compass that can guide you through this wilderness? Enter the world of tarot—a tool not just for soul-searching mystics but for savvy, spirited entrepreneurs like you.

Why Tarot?

Let's address the elephant in the room: skepticism. You're probably wondering, "Tarot cards? For my business?" I get it. Tarot has been pigeonholed as a mystical, woo-woo practice best left for pondering life's existential questions. Until recently, I would have seen this book in a store and thought "that's dumb." But what if it's not dumb?

Here's what I've learned: tarot is like the Swiss Army knife of insight, versatile enough to slice through the fog of personal and professional uncertainty. Tarot isn't a crystal ball that predicts the future; it's more like a mirror reflecting your inner landscape. It won't replace your accountant or your marketing team, but it can offer a new lens through which to view challenges and opportunities. Think of each card as a miniature mentor, offering bite-sized wisdom that can help you navigate the labyrinthine corridors of your business.

The Feminine Touch in Business

You're a woman in the entrepreneurial world, a realm often dominated by testosterone-fueled hustle culture. You're tired of the "grind till you drop" mantra and the relentless pursuit of metrics over meaning. Tarot brings a softer, more intuitive approach to the bottom line. It's like swapping out a sledgehammer for a velvet glove; both can open doors, but one does so with a touch of grace.

What's in the Cards for You

Imagine pulling a card that nudges you to take a risk you've been contemplating but were too afraid to leap into. Or a card that whispers, "Slow down, the world won't crumble if you take a breather." These cards serve as your personal board of advisors, always available at the shuffle of a deck. They can help you dissect your brand's strengths and weaknesses, guide you through tricky negotiations, and even offer a fresh perspective on your marketing strategy.

Your Humble Guide

Think of tarot not as some mystical, far-off concept, but as your new favorite app—right up there with Slack and Canva. I might not be a tarot expert, but when it comes to breaking down big, brainy ideas into bite-sized, easy-peasy chunks? Oh, honey, that's my jam! This book? It's like my personal cheat sheet, my little playbook on the magic of tarot in the business world. So, picture this: I'm the Obi-Wan to your Luke Skywalker, the Giles guiding Buffy through her Slayer journey. I'll spill the beans, show you the ropes, and sprinkle in some magic. But remember, just like in those epic tales, the real power? That's all you, superstar.

Let's shuffle the deck and see what the cards have in store for you.

Tarot 101

The Tarot's Journey from Royal Courts to Your Business Court

Let's take a little time-traveling jaunt, shall we? Picture the Italian Renaissance—a world of lavish feasts, intricate gowns, and courtly intrigues. It's like the "Bridgerton" of the 15th century but with less gossip and more, well, tarot cards. Yep, you heard me right. Before tarot was the go-to for soul-searchers and cosmic wanderers, it was the entertainment du jour for Italian nobility.

From Game Night to Soul Searching

Imagine being at a swanky Italian soirée in the 1420s. You're not discussing the latest episode of "Game of Thrones"; you're engrossed in a card game called "Triumphs." The tarot started as a game, not unlike modern-day bridge, and was all the rage among the Italian upper crust. Forget about ancient Egyptian roots or mystical origins; these cards were more about winning rounds than predicting futures.

The OG Tarot Decks

The Visconti Trumps, created around 1440, are like the "Mona Lisa" of tarot decks—the granddaddies that set the stage for the cards we use today. These decks had four suits with numbers and court cards, plus an extra set of 22 "trump" cards featuring iconic figures like the Pope, the Emperor, and the Wheel of Fortune. Sound familiar? That's because these are the ancestors of our modern Major Arcana.

Tarot Goes Viral

The game of Triumphs was the TikTok dance challenge of its day, spreading like wildfire from Italy to France and beyond. As it traveled, the images on the cards evolved, but the core concept remained the same. It was the ultimate social media trend (minus the social media).

From Poetry to Prophecy

Fast forward to the 16th century, and tarot takes on a poetic twist. Poets used the trump cards as muses to pen verses for the ladies of the court. It's like writing a love song but with tarot cards as your lyrics. By the 18th century, the cards had taken on a more mystical role, like a "Harry Potter" plot twist that no one saw coming.

The Occult Connection

Now, let's talk about the "Stranger Things" of tarot history. In the 18th century, Antoine Court de Gébelin declared that tarot had ancient Egyptian roots. He was convinced that the cards were a "royal road to wisdom," a claim as sensational as any tabloid headline. While this theory has been debunked, it added a layer of mystical allure to the tarot, making it the multifaceted tool we know today.

The Modern Renaissance

Enter the 20th century, and tarot gets a makeover. Edward Waite, a man as enigmatic as Dumbledore, commissioned the Rider-Waite Tarot Deck in 1910. This deck became the "Friends" of tarot—widely loved, easily understood, and globally recognized. And, like "Friends", we can view it now through wiser eyes and recognize that it has some problematic elements, yet familiarity and nostalgia keep us coming back to it. It continues to be the most widely used deck today.

Why Does This History Matter to You?

So, why am I giving you this whirlwind history lesson? Because understanding the tarot's journey helps you appreciate its versatility. It's evolved from a noble's pastime to a poetic muse, and now to a tool for spiritual and business insight. It's like the Madonna of the mystical world, constantly reinventing itself while staying eternally relevant.

So, as you shuffle your deck and lay out your spread, remember: you're not just tapping into your intuition; you're partaking in a rich, ever-evolving tradition. And who knows? Maybe the cards will be the secret sauce that takes your business from startup to empire.

The Ethics of Tarot

The Ethical Compass: Navigating Tarot in the Business Realm

Before I dive into the nitty-gritty of using tarot for your business, let's have a heart-to-heart about the ethical landscape. Imagine you're at a crossroads in your business journey. One path is lit up like a Broadway marquee, screaming "Follow me for guaranteed success!" The other path is softer, illuminated by the gentle glow of fireflies, whispering, "I offer wisdom, not guarantees." Tarot is that firefly-lit path—a guide, not a GPS.

Tarot Isn't Your Business Consultant

First things first: tarot is not a substitute for professional business advice. It's not your accountant, your lawyer, or your marketing guru. Think of tarot as your favorite self-help book. It offers insights and perspectives that can enrich your decision-making process, but it shouldn't be the sole basis for major business moves. It's like adding a dash of cinnamon to your morning latte; delightful but not essential for your caffeine fix.

The Velvet Glove, Not the Iron Fist

Remember, tarot is the velvet glove I talked about earlier. It can open doors to intuitive thinking and offer fresh perspectives, but it's not the iron fist that smashes through obstacles. If you're facing a serious business dilemma—like legal issues or financial crises—consult the experts. Tarot can complement but never replace specialized advice. It's the side dish, not the main course.

The Responsibility is Yours

When you pull a card that suggests taking a risk or making a change, remember that the ultimate decision lies with you. The cards offer a snapshot of potential outcomes, much like viewing a trailer before deciding to watch a movie. They don't absolve you of responsibility for the choices you make. You're the director of your life's film; tarot is just the highlight reel.

Transparency and Team Dynamics

If you're thinking of incorporating tarot into team-building exercises or decision-making processes, be transparent about it. Not everyone is comfortable with tarot, and that's okay. It's like introducing a new Slack channel dedicated to astrology; fun for some but eye-roll-inducing for others. Make it optional and respect diverse opinions.

Don't Play God—or Fortune Teller

Tarot doesn't predict the future; it reflects the present. It's not a crystal ball but a mirror. Using it to make definitive predictions about business outcomes is not just ethically murky; it's misleading. It's like claiming a Magic 8-Ball has the answers to your business strategy—entertaining, perhaps, but not reliable.

The Soulful Approach

What tarot does offer is a soulful approach to business. It invites you to tap into your intuition, to consider alternative viewpoints, and to explore potential paths you might not have considered. It's like having a brainstorming session with your inner self, offering a safe space to ponder, "What if?"

The Final Word

As you shuffle your deck and ponder your next business move, remember that tarot is a tool, not a rule. It's a supplement to your business acumen, a whisper in your ear, not a shout from the mountaintop. Use it wisely, ethically, and in conjunction with solid professional advice, and you'll find it's a valuable addition to your entrepreneurial toolkit.

The Business of Intuition

The Business of Intuition: Unlocking Your Inner CEO with Tarot

Let's talk about that sixth sense we all have but often ignore—intuition. You know, that gut feeling that whispers, "Hey, this is a good idea," or screams, "Run for the hills!" Now, what if I told you that your intuition is like your inner CEO, always ready to offer sage advice, if only you'd listen? And guess what? Tarot can be your boardroom where these high-level meetings with your inner CEO take place.

Intuition: Your Inner Business Consultant

Alan Fine, the genius behind Inside Out Coaching, said it best: "You already know how to be great." Your intuition is that untapped reservoir of greatness. It's not about predicting the future or reading minds; it's about tapping into what you already know. It's like having an internal Google search engine that finds the most relevant answers to your business queries.

Tarot: The Meeting Room for Your Intuition

Think of tarot as a tool that helps you access this innate wisdom. It's not about fortune-telling or predicting stock market trends. It's about creating a space where you can listen to your inner voice, your gut, your intuition—whatever you want to call it. Tarot cards serve as prompts or cues that help you dig deep into your subconscious, like a skilled interviewer coaxing out the real story.

The Synergy of Tarot and Business Acumen

When you lay out a tarot spread, you're essentially setting the agenda for your internal business meeting. Each card serves as a talking point, a subject for discussion with your inner CEO. The cards don't dictate your business strategy; they help you uncover what you already know but may not have consciously acknowledged. It's like sifting through a brainstorming session's Post-it notes to find that one golden idea.

The Art of Tarot and Business

Just as there are different business models and strategies, there are various tarot decks and interpretations. What draws you to a particular deck is often the artwork, much like a company's culture might attract you. The symbolism in the cards resonates with you, enhancing your intuitive connection to the deck. It's like choosing the perfect office décor that stimulates creativity and productivity. The art and cards you'll see throughout this book are from the companion tarot deck "Read The Room: The Entrepreneur's Tarot Deck", but you can use this book with any tarot card deck.

Energy: The Currency of Intuition

When you handle tarot cards, you're infusing them with your energy, your essence. This energy serves as the currency for your intuitive transactions. Some tarot readers prefer not to let others touch their cards to keep the energy "pure," while others welcome the exchange. It's like deciding whether to keep your business meetings exclusive or open to input from various stakeholders.

The Fine Print: Tarot Doesn't Replace Professional Advice

I know I sound like a broken record, but I cannot stress enough that while tarot can offer valuable insights, it's not a substitute for professional business advice. It's a supplementary tool, like a SWOT analysis or a market research report. It can offer a fresh perspective, but it shouldn't be the sole basis for significant business decisions.

Your Intuition, Your Rules

Whether you're a seasoned tarot reader or a curious newbie, the key is to make the practice your own. Take the basics and run with them. Adapt the traditional meanings of the cards to suit your business context. The more you practice, the more you'll find that your readings resonate with your business intuition, making you not just a tarot reader but an intuitive business leader.

Clearing Your Space

Creating a Sanctuary: Clearing Your Space for Focused Tarot Readings

Imagine your mind as a cluttered desk, overflowing with sticky notes, to-do lists, and half-finished projects. Your tarot cards are like a beautiful, blank notebook waiting for you to write your story. But first, you need to clear that desk and create a sanctuary where your intuition can flourish.

The Art of Clearing: Your Deck and Your Space

You've got your shiny new tarot deck, and you're eager to dive in. Hold your horses, lovely! Before you start pulling cards, it's essential to clear both your deck and your reading space of any lingering energies. Think of it as spiritual spring cleaning. You wouldn't cook in a dirty kitchen, so why would you seek spiritual guidance in a cluttered space?

The Many Paths to Clearing

There's no one-size-fits-all approach to clearing your tarot deck and space. It's like choosing a meditation style; what works for one person may not resonate with another. Here are some popular methods to consider:

1. Prayers and Invocations: Call upon higher energies that resonate with you—be it a spirit guide, an ancestor, or the universe itself—to bless your space and deck. It doesn't have to be spiritual. You can call upon the wisdom of Dale Carnegie or the financial savvy of your Meemaw.

2. Singing, Chanting, or Music: Use your voice or favorite tunes to raise the vibration of your environment. Read a poem or a passage from your favorite author. Or keep it simple and blast a playlist that sets the vibe you want.

3. Incense and Smudging: Burn ethically-sourced sage, palo santo, or incense to cleanse the air. It's like giving your space an energy detox. You can spray Florida Water or your favorite body spray. Hell, you can plug in an air freshener - don't over think it.

4. Candles and Lighting: Illuminate your space with candles or soft lighting to create a serene atmosphere. Smart devices make this a lot easier to accomplish. "Alexa, it's time for tarot."

5. Crystals and Talismans: Place power objects like crystals around your space or on your deck to maintain a high energy frequency. Clear quartz and selenite are always good choices for general energy cleaning.

6. Physical Cleaning: Yes, even a good old-fashioned dusting and vacuuming can elevate your space's energy! A cluttered space creates a cluttered mind. So, clear off the piles, file away the paperwork, and turn off electronics. Clean up or put away anything that can become a distraction.

The Power of Intention

No matter how you choose to clear your space, do it with intention. Your actions should serve as affirmations of the space you're creating. It's like setting the table for an important dinner guest; you're making it clear that this space is special.

The Ritual of Maintenance

Just like you wouldn't clean your house once and expect it to stay clean forever, maintaining your tarot space is an ongoing process. Some people like to clear their space before each reading, while others may do it at specific times, like during a new moon. Add a post-it note to your desk, set an alarm on your phone, add it to your calendar, or do all three (I see you ADHD). Listen to your intuition; it will guide you.

The Final Flourish: Charging Your Deck

Once you've cleared your deck and space, take a moment to charge your tarot cards with your energy. Hold them close to your heart, say a few words, or simply sit with them in silence. Again, you can make this as spiritual or practical as you want. You can hunch in the corner and hold the deck in your white-knuckled grasp while whispering "my precious." No judgment. You do you. Just remember that you're not just removing other energies; you're imbuing the cards with your own.

The Major Arcana

The Major Arcana: Your Cosmic Playlist for Life's Big Moments

Ready to dive into the heart and soul of tarot? Let's talk about the Major Arcana, the 22 cards that are like the greatest hits album of your life. These cards are the Beyoncés, the Oprahs, and the Michelle Obamas of the tarot world—powerful, transformative, and oh-so-relatable.

The Archetypal Cast of Characters

Picture the Major Arcana as a star-studded ensemble cast in a blockbuster movie of your life. From the nurturing Earth Mother to the wise Sage, from the Rebel to the Lover, these archetypes are reflections of the roles we all play at different times. They're like the characters in your favorite TV series, each bringing their own flair and drama to the unfolding plot of your existence.

A Picture is Worth a Thousand Words

Each card in the Major Arcana is a mini-movie in itself, filled with symbolic Easter eggs waiting to be discovered. Whether they're numbered from 0 to 21 or just feature evocative imagery, these cards are a visual feast. And don't worry if your deck doesn't have numbers or words; the earliest tarot cards were like silent films, letting the imagery do all the talking.

The Journey of a Lifetime

Think of the Major Arcana as your personal GPS for the soul. Starting with "The Fool," who's like the adventurous backpacker setting off on a world tour, you'll meet a series of guides and challenges along the way. It's a spiritual "Eat, Pray, Love," leading you from innocence to wisdom. Some tarot aficionados even see it as a roadmap to enlightenment, a cosmic curriculum designed to help you discover your truest self.

Not Just Spiritual, But Practical Too

While the Major Arcana does focus on your spiritual journey, it's not all about navel-gazing. These cards also offer real-world advice on everything from family drama to career moves. They're like that wise friend who can talk about both the mysteries of the universe and the latest office gossip with equal enthusiasm.

Your First Steps in Tarot Mastery

If you're new to tarot, the Major Arcana is your starting point, your Tarot 101. Get comfy with these 22 cards, and you'll unlock a treasure trove of intuitive insights. They're the key to understanding the rest of the deck and a powerful tool for self-discovery.

Upright or Reversed: It's All in the Context

When you're doing a reading, pay attention to whether a card appears upright or reversed. But remember, a reversed card isn't necessarily your cosmic "thumbs down." It's all about the context, the surrounding cards, and yes, your own intuitive hits. You're the DJ here, remixing the tarot's symbolism to create a reading that resonates with you.

The Same But Different

For this book, I'm using the Read The Room companion tarot deck. It's based on the Rider-Waite deck, the Taylor Swift of tarot decks—ubiquitous, relatable, and rich in symbolism. Because many tarot decks on the market today are based on Rider-Waite, the descriptions and suggestions here will work with any standard deck.

The Fool

0 - The Fool: The Startup Founder (Ruler: Air)

Upright

Think of The Fool as the Mark Zuckerberg* of your tarot deck—full of untapped potential and ready to disrupt the status quo. This card is all about taking that entrepreneurial leap of faith. It's your "Just Do It" moment, a signal to start that small business you've been dreaming about. But remember, even Zuckerberg had to pivot from his original idea. So, heed the advice: "Look before you leap."

Reversed

In the reversed position, The Fool becomes the Fyre Festival of business endeavors—rash, poorly planned, and doomed from the start. This is not the time for risky business moves or launching new ventures. It's a warning against being the kind of entrepreneur who's all sizzle and no steak.

*We still live in a world where the most ubiquitous and widely recognized examples of certain business concepts and accomplishments are (mostly white) men. Please note that I only include them judiciously to make specific references. Now go shake up the status quo so I can use you as an example in a future addition.

The Magician

I - The Magician: The Sales and Marketing Guru (Ruler: Mercury)

Upright

The Magician is your Don Draper, the master of persuasion and transformation. This card says you've got the skills to bring your business vision to life. It's about aligning all your resources—think SEO, social media, and customer relations—to create something amazing. You're the business alchemist, turning leads into conversions, just like turning lead into gold.

Reversed

Reversed, The Magician becomes the snake oil salesman. You might be talking a big game, but there's no substance behind the words. This is a warning against over-promising and under-delivering, a common pitfall in the world of small business.

The High Priestess

II - The High Priestess: The Strategic Advisor (Ruler: Moon)

Upright

The High Priestess is your Sheryl Sandberg, the COO behind the scenes, guiding you with her intuitive wisdom. This card suggests that you should trust your gut in business decisions. It's also a nod to the importance of data and analytics—the "unrevealed truth" that can guide your business strategy.

Reversed

When reversed, The High Priestess becomes a cautionary tale against ignoring red flags or not doing your due diligence. It's like ignoring market research and then wondering why your product isn't selling. Trusting your gut is good, but ignoring the facts is not.

The Empress

III - The Empress: The Brand Builder (Ruler: Venus)

Upright

The Empress is the Sara Blakely of the tarot world. She's all about creating a brand that people love and trust. This card suggests that now is a great time to invest in your branding and customer experience. Think user-friendly websites, top-notch customer service, and products that make people's lives better.

Reversed

Reversed, The Empress becomes the Elizabeth Holmes of Theranos infamy—a brand built on shaky foundations. This is a warning against cutting corners or being dishonest in your business practices. It could lead to a public relations nightmare.

The Emperor

IV - The Emperor: The CEO (Ruler: Aries)

Upright

The Emperor is the Logan Roy in your deck—ambitious, authoritative, and all about building an empire. This card is a sign that you need to take control, set rules, and create structures within your business. It's about long-term planning and execution, the kind of strategic thinking that turns small businesses into Fortune 500 companies.

Reversed

In the reversed position, The Emperor becomes the Travis Kalanick of Uber—a leader who loses sight of ethical considerations. This card warns against being a dictator rather than a leader. It's a reminder that poor leadership can lead to a toxic work culture and ultimately, the downfall of your business empire.

The Hierophant

V - The Hierophant: The Corporate Consultant (Ruler: Taurus)

Upright

The Hierophant is your McKinsey consultant, the one who brings tried-and-true methods to your business. This card suggests that sticking to established norms and consulting with industry experts could be beneficial. It's the "if it ain't broke, don't fix it" approach. This card could also indicate that your business might benefit from some sort of certification or formal training.

Reversed

Reversed, The Hierophant becomes the disruptive entrepreneur that ignores all the rules and sets new standards. Think Airbnb or Uber—companies that broke the mold and faced backlash for it. This card reversed suggests that it might be time to think outside the box, but warns against becoming the Theranos of your industry—promising big but delivering little.

The Lovers

VI - The Lovers: The Business Partners (Ruler: Gemini)

Upright

The Lovers card is the Ben & Jerry's of your tarot deck—two entities coming together for a common goal. This card suggests that a partnership could be on the horizon. It's also a reminder to balance passion with practicality. Just like in a romantic relationship, in business, it's all about compromise and mutual goals.

Reversed

Reversed, The Lovers become the acrimonious founders who split due to "creative differences." This card suggests that a business relationship could go sour or that a critical decision could lead to a business breakup. It's a cautionary tale to choose your business partners wisely.

The Chariot

VII - The Chariot: The Project Manager (Ruler: Cancer)

Upright

The Chariot is your project manager who ensures that everything runs smoothly. Think of it as your business's NASA launch—careful planning, control, and hard work will lead to success. This card suggests that with focus and determination, you'll overcome any business obstacles.

Reversed

Reversed, The Chariot becomes a failed project or a product recall. It suggests delays, lack of direction, and goals not being met. It's a warning to get back on track and to reassess your business strategies.

Strength

VIII - Strength: The Resilient Entrepreneur (Ruler: Leo)

Upright

Strength is your Martha Stewart, showing that with resilience and emotional intelligence, you can conquer any business challenge (even incarceration). This card suggests that your strength isn't just in your business plan, but in your ability to stay the course when times get tough.

Reversed

Reversed, Strength becomes the entrepreneur who burns out quickly. This card warns against overconfidence and suggests that you may be pushing too hard without sustainable results. It's a reminder to take care of yourself as well as your business.

The Hermit

IX - The Hermit: The Thought Leader (Ruler: Virgo)

Upright

The Hermit is your Brené Brown, the thought leader who steps back to really understand the "why" behind the "what." This card suggests that it might be time for some R&D or a business retreat to reflect on your goals and strategies.

Reversed

Reversed, The Hermit becomes the entrepreneur who never leaves the brainstorming phase, always planning but never executing. This card suggests that while introspection is good, too much can lead to inaction. It's a nudge to stop over thinking and start doing.

The Wheel of Fortune

X - The Wheel of Fortune: The Venture Capitalist (Ruler: Jupiter)

Upright

Think of the Wheel of Fortune as your startup's Series A funding round. When this card shows up, it's like landing a deal on Shark Tank. It suggests a turn of good luck, perhaps an unexpected investor or a sudden market demand for your product. It's the universe's way of saying, "You've paid your dues; here's your break."

Reversed

Reversed, this card is the dot-com bubble burst of your business journey. It warns of setbacks, perhaps a key investor pulling out or a crucial shipment getting delayed. However, remember that downturns are often temporary. It's a cautionary note to have a Plan B and not to put all your eggs in one basket.

Justice

XI - Justice: The Legal Advisor (Ruler: Libra)

Upright

Justice is your business's in-house legal counsel, ensuring that contracts are fair and intellectual property is protected. When this card appears, it suggests that legal matters will go in your favor, whether it's a patent application or a business dispute. It's the "Law & Order" moment where legal expertise saves the day.

Reversed

Reversed, Justice is the courtroom drama you never wanted to be a part of. It warns of legal troubles, perhaps a lawsuit or a failed contract negotiation. It's a reminder to double-check all legal documents and to be cautious in business dealings. In other words, maybe don't call Saul.

The Hanged Man

XII - The Hanged Man: The Pivot Strategist (Ruler: Neptune and Water)

Upright

The Hanged Man is your business's pivot moment, like when Twitter switched from being a podcast platform to a social media giant. It suggests a period of stasis but for a good reason. You might need to sacrifice short-term gains for long-term success. It's the calm-before-the-storm phase of your business journey.

Reversed

Reversed, The Hanged Man is the stubbornness that leads to failure. It's the Blockbuster moment of refusing to adapt to digital media. This card suggests that resistance to necessary change could lead to downfall. It's a warning against complacency and sticking to outdated business models.

Death

XIII - Death: The Rebranding Expert (Ruler: Scorpio)

Upright

Death is your business's rebranding phase, like when Angela Ahrendts steered Burberry from baseball caps to high fashion. It suggests that something old will end for something new to begin. It's not necessarily a bad card; it's the circle of business life.

Reversed

Reversed, Death is the failed rebrand that no one asked for (New Coke, anyone?). It suggests that you're resisting necessary changes, leading to stagnation. It's a warning against being too attached to the past and not innovating for the future.

Temperance

XIV - Temperance: The HR Manager (Ruler: Sagittarius)

Upright

Temperance is your HR department, ensuring that everything is balanced and harmonious. When this card appears, it suggests that a balanced approach will lead to success. It's the "work-life balance" card, reminding you that all work and no play makes Jane a dull babe.

Reversed

Reversed, Temperance is the toxic work environment that leads to high turnover rates. It suggests imbalance, perhaps too much focus on profits and not enough on employee well-being. It's a warning to check in on your team's morale (this includes vendors, freelancers, and supporters) and remember that a happy team is a productive team.

The Devil

XV - The Devil: The Toxic Investor (Ruler: Capricorn)

Upright

The Devil card is like that investor who offers you a deal that seems too good to be true—because it is. This card warns you about the dangers of being seduced by quick money or shortcuts to success. It's the Fyre Festival of your business journey, promising much but delivering little. On the flip side, it could also signify a strong, albeit demanding, commitment like a binding contract that could be beneficial if handled carefully.

Reversed

Reversed, this card is the moment you realize you need to cut ties with that toxic investor or bad business partner. It's your "American Idol" moment when Simon Cowell dons his signature scowl and says "It's a no for me" signaling that it's time to regain control over your business and life.

The Tower

XVI - The Tower: The Market Crash (Ruler: Mars)

Upright

The Tower is the Black Friday of your business—unexpected, disruptive, but potentially clearing the way for something new. It's like a sudden algorithm change that wipes out your website's traffic. While it shakes your world, it also forces you to innovate and adapt.

Reversed

Reversed, this card is the stabilization after the crash. It's the moment you realize that although things were bad, they're starting to look up. It's the post-2008 recovery, slow but steady. However, it could also signify a looming bankruptcy or legal issue that restricts your freedom.

The Star

XVII - The Star: The Influencer Endorsement (Ruler: Aquarius)

Upright

The Star is like getting a shout-out from a major influencer in your industry. It brings hope, visibility, and the promise of future success. It's the viral marketing campaign that takes your small business to the next level. It's the "TikTok effect," where one viral video catapults you into stardom.

Reversed

Reversed, The Star is the bad Yelp review you can't seem to shake off. It's a warning against self-doubt and a reminder that not all publicity is good publicity. It's the cautionary tale of influencer partnerships gone wrong, reminding you to vet your associations carefully.

The Moon

XVIII - The Moon: The Stealth Startup (Ruler: Pisces)

Upright

The Moon is your business in stealth mode. It's the period of uncertainty, where you're not sure if your new product will be a hit or a miss. It's the Apple rumor mill, full of potential but also fraught with misinformation. It's a call to trust your intuition and to be prepared for unexpected opportunities.

Reversed

Reversed, The Moon is the failed product launch that you tried to keep under wraps. It's the Theranos of your business journey, where secrecy and deception lead to downfall. It's a warning against letting your imagination run too wild without grounding your ideas in reality.

The Sun

XIX - The Sun: The Unicorn Startup (Ruler: The Sun)

Upright

The Sun is the moment your startup becomes a unicorn. It's the IPO that turns you into an overnight millionaire. It's the Mansa Musa level of success, where everything you touch turns to gold. It's the ultimate card of success, vitality, and achievement.

Reversed

Reversed, The Sun is the cautionary tale of hubris leading to downfall; where arrogance and misjudgment cloud your vision. It's the moment Icarus realizes the wax is melting. It's a reminder that even at the height of success, one wrong move can lead to a public downfall.

Judgment

XX - Judgment: The Exit Strategy (Ruler: Fire and Pluto)

Upright

The Judgment card is your startup's IPO or acquisition moment. It's the "Shark Tank" pitch where Mark Cuban gives you the nod, and you know you've made it. This card is the ultimate performance review, where all your hard work, late nights, and sacrifices pay off. It's the green light for career moves and indicates that you're in a period of mental clarity, ready to make those big decisions.

Reversed

Reversed, Judgment is the failed IPO or the "Shark Tank" pitch that crashes and burns. It's the indecisiveness that leads to stagnation, like Kodak failing to adapt to the digital age. This card warns you against letting fear and self-doubt cloud your judgment and halt your progress. It's the "WeWork fiasco," reminding you that a lack of decision-making and accountability can lead to your downfall.

The World

XXI - The World: The Global Franchise (Ruler: Saturn)

Upright

The World card is your small business going global. It's the "Starbucks on every corner" level of success. It's the moment when you realize you've built a brand that's recognized and loved, not just locally, but globally. It's the end of one successful venture and the beginning of another, like when Netflix moved from DVD rentals to streaming.

Reversed

Reversed, The World is the franchise that never takes off or the international expansion that fails. It's the "New Coke" mistake, a delay or failure because of poor judgment, bad info, or resistance to change. It's the Blockbuster of your business journey, signaling that you're close to success but warning you not to become complacent or resistant to innovation.

Summary

Think of the Major Arcana as the ultimate board of advisors for your life's startup, a 22-member dream team that's got everything from the visionary (The Fool) to the seasoned CEO (The Emperor) to the disruptor (The Tower). These cards are your cheat codes to leveling up in the game of life, offering gems of wisdom whether you're grinding in the gig economy or aiming to be the next Sarah Blakely.

As you get more XP in the tarot-reading game, you'll start to unlock new achievements and Easter eggs in each card's meaning. Your interpretations will become as customized as a Spotify playlist, fine-tuned to resonate with your unique journey. Whether you're in "hustle mode" like Gary Vee or embracing the Zen of Marie Kondo, the Major Arcana has got a card—and a lesson—for that.

The Minor Arcana

The Minor Arcana: The Ensemble Cast of Your Dreams

Hey, you made it through the Major Arcana—the all-star lineup of coaches, advisors, and CEOs! You're basically halfway through the Marvel Cinematic Universe of tarot cards. But hold onto your seat, because now I'm diving into the Minor Arcana, the unsung heroes of the tarot deck. Think of them as the ensemble cast of "Friends" or "The Office"—each one's got a role to play in the day-to-day drama of your life.

So, what's the deal with the Minor Arcana? Picture them as the episodes in your favorite TV series, filling in the gaps between the season finales and plot twists that the Major Arcana bring. They're the 56 cards that deal with the nitty-gritty, the daily grind, the "Is it Friday yet?" moments. Just like a standard deck of playing cards, they're divided into four suits, each with its own flavor of advice.

The Major Arcana are your go-to for those "OMG, what is the meaning of life?" questions. They're the Gandalfs and Dumbledores, full of ancient wisdom and big-picture advice. On the flip side, the Minor Arcana are your everyday wingmen (or wing-women). Need to know if you should splurge on that new iPhone or stick to your budget? Wondering if it's the right time to slide into someone's DMs? That's where the Minor Arcana come in. They're like the Google Calendar to your life's events, helping you time things just right.

Each suit in the Minor Arcana focuses on a different slice of life. It's like having a playlist for work, workouts, love, and chill time. I won't go card by card—that would be like binge-watching an entire Netflix series in one sitting (tempting, but overwhelming). But I will give you the vibe of each suit and how it can help you make those everyday choices. You know, the ones that don't necessarily make the season finale but are crucial to the plot.

Wands

The Wands Suite

Alright, business moguls and startup wizards, let's talk Wands! Picture Wands as the Gina Boswells and Oprahs of the tarot world—full of fire, ambition, and that "let's change the world" vibe. If the Major Arcana are the C-suite execs, then Wands are your project managers, creatives, and sales dynamos. They're the espresso shot to your Monday morning, the kickstarter to your wildest dreams.

Wands are all about that fire element—think Dragon's Den but less intimidating. In the daily grind of business, Wands are your go-to for anything related to career growth, innovation, and those "light bulb" moments. They're like the Post-its on your vision board, capturing your raw ideas and wildest ambitions. Got a startup idea that you think could be the next Airbnb or Uber? Wands are here to say, "Go for it!"

But wait, there's more! If you're an Aries, Leo, or Sagittarius, you're already vibing with the Wands' fiery energy. You're the kind of person who walks into a meeting and lights it up, both literally and metaphorically. And let's talk timing. In the fast-paced world of business, timing is everything. Wands operate on a "weeks" schedule. So, if you pull the 4 of Wands, you might be looking at a 4-week timeline for your next big launch or project milestone. It's like having a built-in project management tool, but way cooler and more mystical.

So, whether you're scaling the corporate ladder or building your home office empire, Wands are your spiritual LinkedIn, connecting you with the inspiration, determination, and chutzpah to make it happen. They're the ultimate hype squad for your business journey, reminding you that with the right mindset, the sky—or should I say, the C-suite—is the limit!

Cups

The Cups Suite

Calling all rom-com lovers and emotional intelligence gurus, let's dive into the world of Cups! Imagine Cups as the TED Talks that tug at your heartstrings. They're the emotional intelligence (EQ) to your intelligence quotient (IQ), the heart to your mind, the "people person" in your business equation. If Wands are the Steve Jobs of your startup, then Cups are the Brené Browns, bringing empathy, emotional smarts, and a whole lot of love to the table.

Cups are all about that water element—think of them as the spa retreat for your soul, complete with cucumber water and zen playlists. In the 9-to-5 grind, Cups are your HR department, your team-building exercises, and your office parties. They're the emotional glue that holds your business together. They're like the "love react" on your Slack messages, the virtual hugs in your Zoom calls, and the heart emojis in your emails.

Now, if you're a Pisces, Cancer, or Scorpio, you're already swimming in the Cups' emotional waters. You're the person who remembers everyone's birthdays, anniversaries, and even their pet's names. When it comes to timing, Cups don't operate on the clock; they operate on feelings. So, if your reading is chock-full of Cups, you're probably navigating some emotional waters in your business. Maybe it's a partnership that needs reevaluating or a team morale that needs boosting. It's like having a built-in emotional barometer for your business, helping you gauge the emotional climate and act accordingly.

So, whether you're negotiating a merger or planning the office holiday party, Cups are your emotional compass, guiding you through the ups and downs of business relationships. They're the best friends subplot in your corporate drama, reminding you that love, empathy, and emotional intelligence are just as crucial for success as spreadsheets and sales targets. So go ahead, pour yourself a Cup of emotional wisdom; your business will thank you for it!

Pentacles

The Pentacles Suite

Grab your calculators and spreadsheets because we're analyzing the Pentacles suit! Think of Pentacles as the Shark Tank of the Tarot world. They're the Barbara Corcorans, the moguls of material success. If Cups are the emotional heart of your business, then Pentacles are the cold, hard cash and the bricks-and-mortar reality. They're the ROI, the profit margins, and the quarterly reports. They're the bling-bling and the cha-ching of your financial dreams!

Pentacles are all about that Earth element. Imagine them as the fertile soil where you plant the seeds of your business ideas. They're the Tauruses, Virgos, and Capricorns of the zodiac—practical, grounded, and all about that base (no treble). They're the folks who not only look like a million bucks but probably have it in their bank accounts too. And when it comes to timing, Pentacles are all about the long game. They're not your get-rich-quick schemes; they're your long-term investments, your 401(k)s, your real estate portfolios. If your reading is heavy on the Pentacles, you're likely focused on long-term financial goals, maybe even eyeing that early retirement or that dream vacation home.

So, whether you're launching a startup, investing in the stock market, or just trying to balance your budget, Pentacles are your go-to for all things financial. They're the Forbes magazine in your Tarot deck, the Bloomberg Report of spiritual guidance. So go ahead, invest in some Pentacle wisdom; your financial portfolio—and your future self—will thank you!

Swords

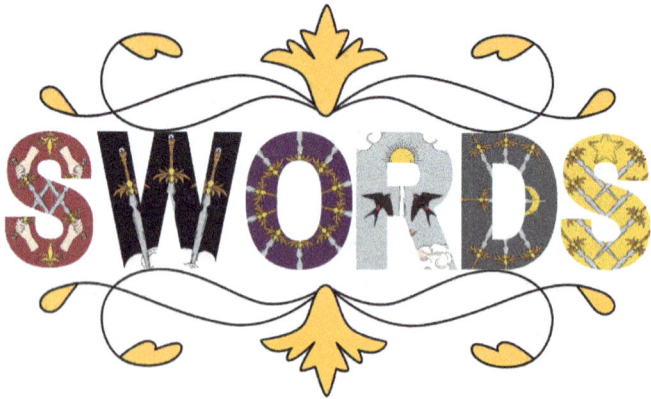

The Swords Suite

Here come the strategic masterminds and corporate ninjas, Swords are the most cutthroat suit of the Tarot deck! If Pentacles are the CFOs, then Swords are the CEOs and COOs, making the tough calls and slicing through the red tape. Think of Swords as the Olivia Pope or Harvey Specter of your Tarot reading—sharp, decisive, and not afraid to play hardball. They're the chess masters, always thinking three moves ahead. They're your SWAT team when things get dicey, and your legal team when you need to negotiate that killer deal.

Swords are all about the element of air—think of them as the Wi-Fi connecting all the departments in your company. They're the Aquarians, Librans, and Geminis of the zodiac—intellectual, analytical, and oh-so-articulate. But be warned, Swords are double-edged. They can cut through confusion to bring clarity, but wielded recklessly, they can also cause chaos. They're the tough love that tells you to pivot or perish.

If you're seeing a lot of Swords in your reading, brace yourself. You're in for some Game of Thrones-level drama and House of Cards intrigue. You might be facing tough decisions, conflicts, or even a full-blown crisis. But don't freak out; Swords are also your reality check. They're the consultants who come in and tell you what's working and what's not. They're the crisis managers who help you navigate through the storm. And when it comes to timing, Swords are your sprinters. They're about quick, decisive action. They're the quarterly sprints, not the long-term strategies.

So, if you're in a high-stakes business environment where decisions need to be made on the fly, Swords are your go-to advisors. They're the McKinseys of your Tarot deck, the crisis PR firms that help you turn challenges into opportunities. So go ahead, draw that Sword card and take command of your business battlefield. Just remember, with great power comes great responsibility. Wield your Swords wisely!

Summary

So there you have it! You're now equipped with a full tarot tool-kit, from the blockbuster hits of the Major Arcana to the indie darlings of the Minor Arcana. It's like having VIP access to the ultimate life festival, complete with headliners and hidden gems. Whether you're navigating the twists and turns of your own personal epic or just trying to make it through another Monday, remember: every card has something to say. So shuffle up, draw, and let's see what the cards have in store for you!

Putting It Into Practice

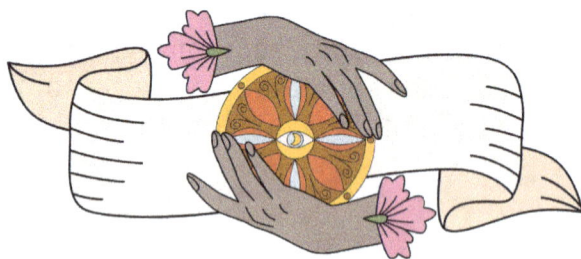

Unlock What You Already Know

Friend, we've reached the end of this magical mystery tour through the Tarot deck. From the Major Arcana's life-altering plot twists to the Minor Arcana's daily grind, we've covered it all. Think of the Major Arcana as the Marvel Cinematic Universe of your life—epic, transformative, and filled with characters that stick with you. On the flip side, the Minor Arcana is like your favorite sitcom—relatable, day-to-day, and oh-so-real.

Together We've explored the Wands, your entrepreneurial mentor, urging you to channel your inner Sarah Blakely. We've swam through the emotional depths of Cups, the rom-com of the Tarot world, where every decision feels like choosing between Ryan Gosling and Ryan Reynolds. Then we counted our Pentacles, the Wall Street tycoons of the deck, reminding you to invest in yourself like you're the hottest stock on the market. And let's not forget Swords, the action heroes and crisis managers, always ready for a duel or a daring rescue mission.

So, what's the takeaway? Tarot isn't just some mystical mumbo jumbo; it's a tool, a roadmap, a mentor, and yes, even a friend. It's like having a coach, a financial advisor, a therapist, and a best friend all rolled into one deck of cards. It's your Dumbledore when you're lost, your General Leia when you're embarking on an adventure, and your Oracle when you need wisdom. As you shuffle those cards and lay them out, remember, you're not predicting the future; you're creating it. Each card is a choice, an opportunity, a lesson. So go ahead, draw your cards and play your hand. Whether you're chasing dreams, or building empires, your Tarot deck is your co-pilot, your scriptwriter.

Thanks for joining me on this Tarot trek. May your cards be ever in your favor!

The Entrepreneur's Compass Tarot Spread

1

Strength

5

External

6

Hidden

N

4

Threat

W

1

Outcome

E

2

Weakness

S

Opportunity

3

When it comes to making business decisions, Tarot can offer valuable insights and perspectives that you might not have considered. Here's a specialized Tarot spread designed to help you navigate the complexities of the business world. I call it the "Entrepreneur's Compass Spread."

This spread consists of 7 cards laid out in the shape of a compass, with each direction representing a different aspect of your business decision.

1. North - Strength: Place this card at the top. It shows the skills, talents, or resources you have that can aid you in this decision. This is your business toolkit.

2. East - Weakness: Place this card to the right of the Outcome card. It represents the gaps in your strategies for achieving the best outcome. This is your mentor or business coach, calling out your bullshit.

3. South - Opportunity: Place this card at the bottom. It reveals the opportunities that could arise from your decision. It is the open door leading you to new possibilities.

4. West - Threat: Place this card to the left of the Outcome card. This represents the challenges or obstacles you might face. This is the metaphorical "glass ceiling."

5. Northwest - External Influences: This card sits between the North and West cards. It highlights external influences that could affect your decision, like market trends or competitors. It's your industry news update.

6. Northeast - Hidden Factors: This card sits between the East and North cards. It uncovers hidden factors or blind spots you should be aware of. It's the fine print in your business contract.

7. Center - The Outcome: Place this card in the center. It represents the potential outcome of your decision. Is it the pot of gold at the end of the rainbow or a storm cloud on the horizon?

To use this spread, shuffle your Tarot deck while focusing on your business question. Draw the cards randomly and place them in the positions as described. Take your time interpreting each card, considering how they interact with each other to give you a 360-degree view of your business decision.

Remember, Tarot is a tool for insight and guidance. Always use your own judgment and consult with professionals when making significant business decisions. Happy reading!

The Business Quick-Check Spread

For those days when 'life moves pretty fast', here's a simple yet insightful classic 3-card spread tailored for everyday business decisions. I like to call this one the "Business Quick-Check Spread."

1. Card 1 - Situation: This card represents the current situation or the decision you're facing. Think of it as the "elevator pitch" of your dilemma. It gives you a snapshot of what you're dealing with right now.

2. Card 2 - Action: This card suggests the action you should take. Imagine this card as your business consultant for the day, offering you a single, actionable piece of advice.

3. Card 3 - Outcome: This card shows the likely outcome if you follow the advice from the Action card. Consider this your "profit forecast," giving you a glimpse into the future returns on your actions today.

To use this spread, focus on your question or decision while shuffling your Tarot deck. Draw three cards and lay them out from left to right in the order mentioned. Take a moment to reflect on each card and how they relate to each other.

This 3-card spread is like the Google search of Tarot readings—quick, easy, and perfect for answering those everyday business questions. This spread can offer valuable insights in a jiffy.

Remember, while Tarot can offer intriguing perspectives, it's not a substitute for professional business advice. Use it as a tool for reflection and inspiration as you navigate the business landscape. Happy reading!

Acknowledgements

I believe in transparency and not gate-keeping, so I'd like to acknowledge that this book would not exist with out the following people, places, and things.

Canva, Creative Market, Chat GPT, the dozens of tarot guides and decks strewn about my office, way too much coffee, a fuckton of research, and my bestie/collaborator, Laura.

About the Author

Robyn Sayles is the Founder/Brand Strategist for Launching Your Success and the Showrunner/Co-Host of the Unf*ck My Business Podcast (soon to be a book). After spending 20+ years working for big ol' corporations she now works with creative entrepreneurs, polymaths, and misunderstood genius types helping them turn their crazy ideas into captivating content.

She lives in Florida with her husband, two kids, and two dogs. And, like many of you, she went through some shit during the COVID pandemic and entered into 2023 with a broader perspective, narrower priorities, significantly less fucks to give, and a burning desire to do all those things she was always scared to do including writing books.

More information, links, and resources can be found at www.robynsayles.com.